I Weave a Nest of Foil

I Weave a Nest of Foil

POEMS

Arlene Naganawa

kelson
books

Portland, Oregon
David Oates, General Editor

Published by Kelson Books
2033 SE Lincoln
Portland OR 97214

kelsonbooks@gmail.com

Cover art: Rickie Wolfe
Cover and interior design: Steve Connell | *steveconnell.net*

Printed in the USA

ISBN 979-8-218-32090-4

Library of Congress Control Number: 2023951105

Contents

I

Tell You What

CVS

I had given up the material world
but was tempted by snacks in cellophane bags.

I searched for thin places where the spirit
might find me, where angels might touch

my blue dress. Plastic cups lined a counter:
gold, translucent red. I ran my finger round

the lips, as if a sacrament. I could hardly
believe the bounty, aisles wide and clean,

shelves of hair ties and Kleenex. Surely God
must enter through the automatic doors.

Outside, rain blustered through the trees.
Inside, only sounds of customers

dropping mints and toothbrushes
into their baskets, shuffle

of soles on linoleum. The sky
flicked white, electric.

I WEAVE A NEST OF FOIL

The night is sweet as powdered sugar, rotting porches.
I dream a bayou where cypresses turn to firs.

The crescent moon is a jewel I drink in my chicory.
My hands glow at the moment of fortune.

Guns fire near my street, cries like confetti.
Gaslight, ghost light. My bodies always disappear.

I WRITE TO YOU IN ISOLATION

Numbers fall like rain-soaked leaves on river rock.
(How many ripples complete a pond?)

Ice on bruised eyelids.
Scrim of frost on a glass door.
That was today's time.

But chicks peck out under hens in my storybook.
We aren't sick, not yet.
Do you feel them, the pick pick?

FOR THE QUEEN OF KINDNESS

1

I made a wreath of leaves,
each leaf a light.

Burgundy and lime, dry and tender.

A breathing forest floor.
A flicker knocking.

A funnel web I didn't recognize.
Sunlight drove into the rocks

rose but with a yellow in it.

2

We wrote into each other's lines
like sisters

our poems of other worlds.

3

Lily wilting like wet silk.
Candles listless and unbearable.

*You protected yourself
and loved small.*

I sealed a nickel in a walnut shell.
I made a lemon into a pig,

cloves for luck, penny cut
into its silent jaw.

The stone. The flower.

The snail, softly.

A TIME

1

There was a time when a deer came out of the trees on the side of
     the road
and I was driving alone and I had not been driving alone for very
     many months

and the deer, silvery and large, stepped out in the beam and
     someone inside me
asked if I were afraid to die and the fog came toward me like a
     ghost.

2

My mother said, *If you don't have anything nice to say don't say
     anything,*
but she said not-nice things, so many that I had to close my ears.

My dog, who was not our dog, listened well, lay on the rag rug,
     slept
most of the day while my mother ironed out wrinkles.

3

A girl carried a sand pail and a shovel. Yellow whales swam on
     the bib
of her sunsuit. The real sun glowed over her head. Her shoulders
     burned

like kisses blister, sticky popsicle red.

4

I was walking up the road that passed the white house hidden
        behind
the wire gate entwined with vines and a crushed-in Chevy in the
        yard

when the sun touched the top of my hair and a little red garter
        snake
uncurled near my toes.

5

I dreamed of a tapir in the underbrush, breathing out, lowering
        his eyelashes.
Inside the deep cavern of his sleep, he saw no moon, no stars,

having never looked up to the fluttering sky, but always down
to leaves trampled under his hooves.

6

The sun and moon appeared simultaneously in the sky.
I saw this through my windshield tissued with spinners fallen
        from maples.

I saw a man half-under a laurel; the body turned gray. The
        policemen
looked up for the moon and then down Pine.

7

Shelling peas from the market, I saw why shells were called so,
crisp shells in the boathouse, oars lifting like fins skimming the
        waves.

Racing shells, shells to protect, shells dropped in a pot, boiled.

8

I was waking, my roof awash with rain after snow. Outside, the
        tall tree
sheltered a peppering of birds and a cloud cover soft as tea steam.

Tracks circled the face of the clock and I faced it.

9

My windshield shivered with snow. And the deer, large and
        silver,
passed slowly through the fenced pasture.

A STORY

The lighthouse keeper folds his blanket, waits for the return of
      his beloved
who has floated over or sunk below the furls of the sea, always
      the sea.

But there is only the lift of terns over the thrift gone purple in
      the crevices
between rocks scattering the backshore, sand left whisperless

and his breath so quiet that even the hiss of a kettle seems a
      storm.
Gulls strut the darkest sand exposed when the tide pulls out.

He thinks, there are miracles. But this is not his story,
not the one where the starfish rises in the sky on a cold night

or the good man finds his love, her shining fins turned to limbs.
In this account, there is no man, no gentle beauty. The light goes
      out.

Wind rushes up the bluff. Gulls scatter like paper napkins.

SPACE BEAR, HEAVEN AND EARTH

Tlingit artist, Alison Marks

In October 2000, American astronaut William Shepherd flew
a Tlingit bear mask into space aboard the Russian Soyuz spacecraft.
(Italicized lines from Alison Marks' and Paul Marks' *Heaven and
Earth*)

A thin dog-dream comes in a fog.
I feed it scraps of oranges.

It follows me in the street
and into the forest.

It does not roll forward in orbit
like the quiet Russian dog

whose heart the men burned in space.
A star, its own distant word—

so small, it dies like a cub.
A sacrifice. I knew about that.

The dream-dog whispers in my ear:
They said this to trap him, so that they could accuse him.

I knew about this. I know about that.

INTERROGATIVE

I'd like to say candlelight.
And a wolf's long legs like saplings.

Frost stippling the lawn.

I was there, pensive, waiting out
the dark.

My hands singeing my hair.

CREATION

Wolf on the crest.

Streams dry as dropped ribbon.

Shred of cloud like a tablecloth
spread open, dusted with sugar.

The moon, wasted over the pasture,
wasted like milk, like milkweed mown over.

ONE AFTERNOON

We left our bikes, both of us, for the secret
place, forest on a cliff, dim and fresh
with paths and a cave of fallen branches.

There we were *we*, a beginning
like an underground stream bubbling to surface
too clear for tadpoles, though we wanted it

wanted it to be something *becoming*:
whole robin egg, shed snakeskin,
mouse skull, perfect and clean.

INVITATION

ghosts linger in the pass-through

let them sleep in our bed

let them roll in mothy complications

let them turn their faces to our faces

let them give us their icy handshakes

let them open like flashlights

let them turn bedsheets into pages

let them scribble goodwill wishes

THE WHITE STONES

She imagines a pocketful of stones. She imagines while crows
       tatter the air
on shoulders, and light drifts downstream. He imagines a year
       without speaking—

silence forms a hole in his throat. Geese slide a V under power
       lines, a wave
on a wintry pond. He fingers a coin in his jacket pocket. Now: a
       shining moment,

one she could turn back to. She thinks about smoking, blood-
       sigh of valves and tissue
thin leaves of a magazine she could have subscribed to,
       pretending. He had hoped for

the slam of a screen door, cloud of mosquitoes, cry of swallows
       when day falls
like a lover's coat. Luminous and remembered: shadows spilled
       on a riverbank,

a pool of rain, stiff sparrow wrapped in white tissue, fist-sized
       gift left in the earth.

SELF-PORTRAIT AS A NUMBER OF THINGS

Piccola. On Christmas morning
the barn swallow appeared
in the poor girl's wooden shoe.

Her joy filled me with pine needles.
My favorite story insists
I wanted to save everyone.

I wanted to be a mother.
I wanted to be a just god.

NO ONE PRAISES ORDINARY

It's usually dim here, anyway.
Fog blurs our imperfections. Don't you miss
the magic of the darkroom, chemicals
and negatives, the slow appearance of faces?

The highway is ugly but beautiful.
The joy of getting from one place
to the next and another next from there.

TELL YOU WHAT

Inspired by "State of Being (Boats)" and "In the Hand"
by Chiharu Shiota

1

I like how you encased your organs in a box.
A tangle of arteries and watercraft.
You can examine them whenever you please
without taking off your clothes or cutting yourself open.

2

I like how your dresses fled the cabinets.
The puffed skirts, cakes of desire.
And the absence of hands, of heads.
The single beds, raveling.

3

I like when I close my eyes
strands materialize like a scrub pad
in my palm where a sudsy bird might rest
for a minute before drowning.

SURPRISE

The sun was so bright last summer.
We ate crackers on the patio.

The surprise was a dove
mourning in the oak tree.

A soft landing.
I thought it would disappear,

fleeting, the way a stranger
will tell you his saddest night.

I expected nothing to happen,
not this year, not the next.

NO ONE KNEW TO LOOK FOR ME

Finally moss began to grow.

Trees stretched.
The lifeboats emptied.

The limbs splayed like insects.
Exhalation of leaves,

lanterns blown.
The night, so cold.

I left my clothes in the branches.

THE NAMING

It was privilege to name the things —
the crawling and the vining
the swimming and the ones that bloomed
when we opened our hands.

We took it seriously — St. John's wort and supplejack
stickleback and funnel weavers, drizzle, whirlwinds.
Roosevelt and the elk christened with his name.
We named, we claimed.

We started early. The stars a million years
beyond our world, the numbers that swirled
around us: exponents, square roots, zero. Organs
and illnesses, words for things our bodies do,

heavenly and otherwise. We were so wise.
But in our dreams, we refuse. Clouds (not *clouds*)
drift slowly by, animals wander near, all teeth and fluff.
And the lovers — just *honey baby you there.*

IF YOU ARE LUCKY

If you are lucky in this life
a hen's egg will appear in your palm.
If you are lucky, someone

you love will have placed it there.
All over the country
napkins fall like wings in the dark.

When candlelight falls,
someone you love
will place the goblets, no matter

how long since she or he
has departed. If salt spills,
spelling good fortune,

it's a gift on the open leaves.
You may remember the moon
cradles all orphans.

Rain will wash the clean part
in your hair, and your hands
cup to receive it.

II

This Dream Has a Trapdoor

SHE DEALS

slipping the knave
from her sleeve.

He conjures a rabbit
in white-gloved air.

This dream, they whisper,
has a trapdoor.

Many tricks,
old and enticing.

Here, you can cut a life in two—
she fans open

her knife bouquet—
or mend it.

IN THIS HEAT I THINK OF LOLITA

If some cafe sign proclaimed Ice Cold Drinks,
she was automatically stirred,
though all drinks everywhere were ice-cold.

Ice-cold lip of the glass
in another vinyl booth, my thighs bare,

shivery at the edge
of the misremembered lake, toes

under a cold skim at the end
of summer. First time, so many firsts—

first bath, first gash in the back
of my head, washcloth red

in the backseat of the sedan.
First night in a strange bed,

neon flickering *Vacancy,*
cold pop in the machine

in the office, half-read magazines,
ashtrays filled and waves

rising from the asphalt parking lot.

MY FRIEND TOLD ME

her mother's secret to washing plates was the wrist.
Her mother's kitchen shone like a waxed Cadillac.

We were eating meatloaf on patterned dishes
in the dining nook when my friend's father called her

a little slut. *Bonanza* flickered in the living room.
My friend told me she didn't want

her headstone to say *She was clean.* Her mother died
and then her father. A few years later,

I rinsed the dishes in my boyfriend's sink,
unwrapped pink Hostess Snoballs

on his waterbed. I remembered the strangeness of sweet
pickle chips, Miracle Whip on soft bread.

WE WANTED BILLY, EVEN THOUGH

his face was spotted like grease soaking the white paper
we packed fries in. He was the only boy in the off-the-highway-

chicken-in-a-basket-picnic-table-out-front drive-in
favored by ants and sparrows. We pestered *what was he up to*

and some of us really wanted to know,
like was he cruising his Chevy round the Loop

and would one of us be chosen
to flip our hair out the window on that hot endless night?

Our lives were sticky—counters, spatulas, foreheads under our
        bangs.
You'd think a person would get sick of burgers and soft serve

when we got as much as we wanted but our skirts
felt tighter every day. No one good ever came in,

just sweaty moms carrying kids and a few grannies and gramps
driving through, the old guy in black socks and bermudas,

his wife toting a straw purse with seashells glued on.
Older boys from our brothers' class were slogging through

swamps; names like Mekong murmured from televisions left on
during dinner, Cronkite over pot roast and milk, flames too far
        away

to touch us. Days were cheeseburgers wrapped in square foil,
counting dimes for change, waiting by the phone.

Newspapers landed on our steps but except for Dear Abby
we didn't read them, just looked at photos so distant

they could've been shadows on the moon.
Mosquitoes drank their fill over there and here

as we lay alone in our twin beds, porch lights on,
feeling the curtains lift and turn in the dark.

ARE THEY JAUNTY?

Are they a nice bird?
Are the people who like them cheerful?

Are their bright red check marks in the snow
reminders there was once goodwill,

a fire in a hearth for toasting bread
on an iron fork? Are their wings a tip

of blood, accident from the cup,
whip wound, gunshot, holy snow?

TODAY

the rabbits have gone a little wild

hummingbirds dip like jets

the cloud I saw was a mashed potato

she told me she saw an owl in a tree in a city park and I was
        jealous
she told me the cloud looked like a horse
she told me her hair was a waterfall and quoted a prism
she told me ashes fell like salt on her skin

MI VIDA LOCA

he shows me
his new tattoo: three dots
under his left eye

and on his inner wrist:
a scar like lips
the blood like spilled ink

(the spilt milk—
palm held to the searing
cast iron pan

greased with bacon,
eggs with fluttery edges thrown
to the door)

three dots like sharp pops
from the intersection
like buttons to press

my fingers to
like tears
like little kisses

THE WEEK

A Russian skater and threats to Ukraine.
On my desk, an azure marble etched
in gold—a tiny globe—clear as the irises

of the girl who gave a present to her teacher
with the pull-down world map—*here is Russia,*
we are here. Clear as the sky that holds

the bombs, clear as the bell that clangs
inside the skater's head each time she stumbles.
The tiny continents are traced in gold

like flecks in a cat's eye. Inside the circle,
the shooter tocks, the timer ticks, one minute
in the long program.

THE BODIES

Lips sealed, he tells them.

Shooting stars are not the same as shooting.
Scissors slice the Latin: *cut, kill—decide, decide.*

Sunlight hits the playground.
Lights out. They'd practiced.

He wonders, who are they? outside? in here?
See, it happens—

Know, not know—the hollow of the mouth.
They hear what they hear.

A child holds his knees.
A child sees dust.

THE DOOR

A door opened into her body.
Her fingers dimmed.

So this is someone's work, she thought,
the dimpled spider and the white heal-all.

Her heart waned in the cave.
A fox crept to the mouth, lowered his head.

Wind shivered through her gown.
Where is he going? she asked.

At night flowers closed
like ghosts on their stems,

moth wings ruined by fingers. Voices floated
from the hall, lungs filled and emptied,

alveoli like paintbrush bracts,
like tips of lit torches.

I WOULD FOLLOW SUCH BEAUTY ANYWHERE

I thought about why I could not speak, my tongue
cut out so long ago I remembered it only as a plum

in my mouth, golden and fleshy, sentences like leaves
or hoof beats. I thought about thought and how

others must enter the soft sky of their thinking,
their thoughts the color of salamanders or streams.

My thoughts were transparent, black framed, edged
in obsidian chips, and then I was away on a prairie

that I'd seen once or remembered from a book.
My eyes were silver and there was a wind unfolding

from the east with clouds threading through magpies.
I thought about elk, their cold hoof-breath,

their flanks like water, a calf bleating in a cave,
a wolf, suspended in mid-air, mouth wide open.

THE GIRL

Like teeth in a jar, fears collect over years: cries from
the other riverbank, hearts like two moons under one skin.

Every time I climb into the boat, someone says a prayer.
Each dip of the oar is newborn and finished, all at once.

Every bird song is farewell, every inland tide a miracle.
Bear devours the moon. Whatever has crawled into the cave

sleeps there: Ursa Major for me; perhaps, for you, a dragon
or a little bear breathing softly in its dreams. I walk toward you,

Cave. Open your mouth, take my bare skin, my ragged bundles.
Take my eyes like birds destroyed by flames.

THREE SCARECROWS DELIVER HUCK FINN

1

Child, you know
you are one of us:
scraps of ragbag, whiskey,
yards of dust and despair.
Our hearts are cornhusk
and frying pan;
yours bittersweet, blood
pumped with a feather pen.

Come sit among the ruby tomatoes,
taste the sharp juice,
seeds spilling over your chin.
We conjure poppies to fly
like scarlet parrots, pirates' birds,
eyes obsidian, deep
as bayou midnight.

We jangle charms on our branch
and broomstick wrists,
call forth bats
to rattle the night's wind.

2

A barn owl's wide eye
sees the moon's coin-toss,
spin of silver reeling
down a man's dark path.
Yours we feel under the flat soles
of our invisible feet.

3

Who is she, this Becky Thatcher
whose mouth suggests cardinals and hollyhocks,
whose eyes reflect lantern light?
Who is he, this Tom who played hide
in the land of the dead
and sauntered home again,
whose face death did not wizen,
whose eyes did not darken
but shine, fireflies
of youthful cruelty?

These two are mute,
patchwork child.
The dead can be only deaf,
shadows in the cave.

4

Now sky, frost, fish-
belly white. Your Pap waits
behind vines of ropy hair.
He wants your sack of silver.
He wants to swallow,
squeeze your heart.

Crows rise from stones,
preen their oily tail feathers,
strut the aviary of avarice.
See how greed's talons
sweeten the vines, how tin
sparkles in its curved beak.
Put your naked feet
on the ground, child:
one path is lined with crows,
the other, glittering blackbirds.

5

Do you miss
your mother, Huck?
Her hand to smooth your face,
to comb your baby locks?
Where are lilacs
and forget-me-not?
Whose songs float
through your nightmares,
tear webs from the stars?

6

Two chambers hollow your heart:
river fills one,
stars bumping a towhead,
yolk of moon in an eddy.
Wings fill the other,
owl cry at twilight, empty sky
where you traded the coin
of your soul for Jim's freedom,
weighted your heart with a stone,
let his unfold pinions.

Jim who praised the Lord,
steered the raft, who knew
what a man could not stand;
who could not rise
in the parlor or face of law;
could not raise his own child,
but rowed beside you, orphan,
in clear Southern moonlight;
who believed that a hairball
from an ox's fourth stomach
could foretell the future;
that the moon laid the stars.

What good has it done
to know that the moon
has no breast or heartbeat?

Men still set dogs on fire,
still grin through their pickets of teeth.

7

What hell awaits a sinner?
Innocent, do you fear
who you might find there?
Will you be forced to your knees
to mutter over your supper,
will a body wash up in the reeds?

Ragtag boy, we're all
the same cloth,
seed flung to wind.
Those are gunshots in the distance.
Weeds spill into daylight.
Glass rubies glitter in our hair.

I RECEIVE

my baby girl, wrapped in a cotton
swaddle. The ghost moves close,

and the baby becomes the mother
of the shadowy sadness that is motherhood,

death lurking behind birth,
soft powder of skin faint as breath

ruffling the edge of sleep.
The infant ghost sits up before God,

hopeful, the Word, but oh how strong
does a mother have to be?

DIARY

I see an autumn leaf
and it breaks my heart.

My job is to sweep.
I whisk feathers

and scattered petals.
A nearby creek

fills with clouds.
I feed the birds—

finches and the parakeets.
I wonder if leaves

of books
are scented hyacinth.

MADELINE

When I was a boy
she said

I held field mice
in the curl

of my fingers
dropped rocks

other boys
pitched

at garage doors
in the dark.

I asked
for the bitterest

tea, prayed
I could learn

to charm bees
to be honey.

I was a windfall
wild apple

wasp trapped
in foxglove

I was still
as a lake

frozen
over.

MY MUG FROM JAPAN SAYS
ENJOY THE HAPPINESS TIME

What is the vine blooming outside the door?

My friend's face, a sun from another world.

And something so far away,

a mountain covered in blue flowers.

DEATH, PERFECT

a stillness
will appear in your body

in the ravines and hollows
the sunlight filling

(a breath
we had not noticed—

trill of a little wren)

this will be the present
you've waited for

without knowing
leaves detaching

one by one

stems silent
(the winter trees)

WATER

Bones splinter under lights.
In the moving car, shattered things jangle.
I stare through the window, hold my fingers
to my mouth. I had wanted to be a nurse,
someone with a needle to suture bloody grins
opened unexpectedly on legs, on abdomens.

I thought I could learn the miracle of transfusions.
Instead, I entered a forest where birds flickered
through silence. A fallen fir, crumbling, lay at my feet,
a nurse log, fungi rising like ghosts from her trunk.
Her bones were soft, melting, blanketed with ferns.

Someone told me, *Lift the bodies from the leaves,*
from deep water. You, there, receive the crushed sockets,
the latticed, shiny scars.

NOTES

"Tell You What" and "No One Knew to Look for Me" are based on art by Chiharu Shiota.

"For the Queen of Kindness" was inspired by Toni Morrison.

"Self-Portrait as a Number of Things" was influenced by Maged Zaher.

"Space Bear, Heaven and Earth" is based on a painting by Allison Marks and an installation at the Frye Museum by Allison Marks and Paul Marks.

"If You Are Lucky" contains a line from "Lucky" by Tony Hoaglund.

"In This Heat I Think of Lolita" begins with an epigraph by Vladimir Nabokov.

Mi Vida Loca is a tattoo.

"The Week" was written in February, 2022, during the Winter Olympics and prior to Russia's invasion of Ukraine.

"The Door" contains a line from Robert Frost's "Design."

"My Mug from Japan says *Enjoy the Happiness Time*" contains a line from *Obit* by Victoria Chang.

ACKNOWLEDGMENTS

Thank you to the following journals and presses for publishing these works, sometimes in different forms:

All the Sins: "I Would Follow Such Beauty Anywhere"

Barnstorm: "The Door" (as "The Heart")

Caketrain: "She Deals"

Diner: "The White Stones"

Fatal Flaw: "Tell You What"

La Piccioletta Barca: "Death, Perfect," "For the Queen of Kindness"

Pontoon: "Creation"

Private Graveyard, Chapbook, Gribble Press: "One Afternoon," "The White Stones"

Telephone: "I Write to You in Isolation"

The Ark and the Bear," Chapbook, Floating Bridge Press: "A Time," "The Girl," "We Wanted Billy, Even Though"

The Inflectionist Review: "I Weave a Nest of Foil"

The Seattle Review of Books: "La Vida Loca," "The Door" (as "The Heart")

Waxwing: "Water," "Space Bear, Heaven and Earth"

We Were Talking about When We Had Bodies: Triple Series Chapbooks, Ravenna Press: "A Story," "Are They Jaunty?" "For the Queen of Kindness," "I Would Follow Such Beauty," "I Write to You in Isolation," "Interrogative," "My Friend Told Me," "Self-Portrait as a Number of Things," "Space Bear, Heaven and Earth," "Tell You What," "The Door" (as "The Heart"), "The Naming," "The Week," "Today"

IN GRATITUDE

I am grateful for John Sibley Williams who kindly selected and guided this manuscript.

I am continually thankful to my writing community—Samar Abulhassan, E. Briskin, Chris Crew, Raanan David, John Davis, Barbara Erwine, Marcene Gandolfo, Sharon Hashimoto, Karen Holman, Fredda Jaffe, Greg Jensen, Rachel Karyo, Miho Kinnas, Susan Landgraf, Bob McNamara, Deb Moore, Jeanne Morel, Sati Mookherjee, Arlene Plevin, Kathryn Rantala, Sarah Rauch, David Spataro, Michael Spence, Ann Spiers, Anthony Warnke, John Willson, Melody Wilson, and Deborah Woodard.